Whole Heart Social Media Success Formula™

What to Say, Where to Play, How to Win

Intentional Social Media For Purpose-Driven Entrepreneurs

By

By Diana Concoff Morgan, M.A., HHE

Disclaimer: Facebook, LinkedIn, and all other Social Media platforms mentioned in this book are registered trademarks. Unless otherwise noted, the author is not associated with any product or vendor mentioned in this book. Neither Facebook, LinkedIn, nor any other social media platform mentioned in this book endorse any material.

Contents

C. Start Increasing Your Visibility

Part VII: Use Social Media To Inspire And Motivate

Conclusion

DEDICATION

To my son, Zach, whose birth inspired me to quit my corporate job to become an entrepreneur so I could be present in his life. And to my mom for always loving me unconditionally. And to my late husband, Dindayal, who always encouraged me to take the most significant leaps and stood behind me.

ACKNOWLEDGMENTS

Thank you to everyone who helped me along the way with this book. So much gratitude to my soul sisters: Cyndee Paulson Heer for inspiring me to discover my purpose, which led to writing this book; Gail Blasie for her unwavering support and encouragement; Colleen Grim for her sparks of inspiration throughout the years and throughout the writing of this book, Kim Bergman, PhD, Natalie Bergman, and Amanda Slade for always encouraging me to stand in my power. Thank you to my coach, mentor, and soul sister, Catarina Rando, for always holding the biggest vision of possibility for me. Thank you to Michael Thomas Peterson, Davey Baranco Brown, and Alan Brown for your motivation and inspiration. Thank you to Elana Feldman, Lynn Lambrecht, and Jennie Jolly for your words of wisdom and your expertise in reading, editing, and feedback.

PREFACE

This book evolved from my passion for helping heart-centered, purpose-driven entrepreneurs learn how to use the Internet to make an impact. My goal is two-fold. First, I offer you 17 years of the tried and tested strategies I have used and taught my clients. These are "evergreen" strategies, meaning they will work no matter how the social media landscape evolves. Please read through this book and then use it as a guide. Implement these strategies to grow your visibility, influence, impact, and your business! Second, I hope my story will inspire you to take the risk to become more visible. I share my story because, maybe, I was you, the introvert, the shy person who existed behind the scenes, watching all those people who could just "put it out there" while wishing I could do that. It seemed so easy for them. I'm here to tell you that you don't have to be that person to create an authentic and monetizable online presence. You can be yourself and grow a following and a thriving business on social media!

"I have a vision of a world of compassion and love where all people of all generations are inspired and empowered to connect and share their hearts!"

May you reach the people who need you and manifest the healing and transformation you came here to for yourself, your family, your community, and the world.

PART I

The Power of Social Media

"Through social media, we can spread awareness, foster community, and ignite global movements for a healthier planet." ~ Leah Thomas

Introduction - My Why

Have you ever considered deleting your social media? When I was about 3, my brothers, 4 ½ and 6, used to chase me around the house. I would run as fast as my little legs could carry me. When I got tired, I would stop and lie down on the floor, face down, and hide my eyes from them. They would stop chasing me, so I thought they were gone. When I got up, they would pounce on me! Social media is just like that! *You can run, but you can't hide!*

It's not that we don't like social media; it's that we don't like what people sometimes do with social media. Social media can be harmful, superficial, ridiculous, and even hurtful. But it can also be a powerful force for creating positive change in the world!

"Every sweet hath its sour." Ralph Waldo Emerson

~

"Knowledge is Power." Thomas Jefferson

~

"Let's elevate the quality of social media to use social media to elevate humankind." Diana Concoff Morgan

~

I aim to inspire you to elevate your message on social media to grow your brand and legacy as an expert and grow your business. I hope you will start embracing social media, enjoy it, share your message, and make a more significant impact.

1.2

My Story

I've always been on a mission to inspire people to have a voice, share their message, and be seen and heard. That has been my purpose since I emerged from feeling powerless, silenced, and invisible as a child. Once I found my voice, I never lost my passion for giving that gift to others!

Trained as a teacher in my early 20s, I was seduced away from teaching by a 10-year corporate career. I refer to myself as a recovered corporate misfit. I didn't fit into the corporate culture and felt silenced again. It wasn't my path or my world. When I became a mom, I was changed forever. My son came home from school one day complaining that he hated school. That was the turning point. I realized I needed to be there for him and became an entrepreneur. That way, I would have the flexibility and freedom to be there for my son, continue fulfilling my life purpose, and generate an income.

I had been officiating spiritual rites of passage ceremonies for friends and family. I felt it was a calling but never saw it as a business. After attending one of those "self-actualization" seminars, I declared that I would quit my job in 6 months. The opportunity came up much sooner than I had planned (careful what you pray for). I was out of there for a month! So, I decided to do it! I turned my hobby into a business, which became my calling. I returned to school, got my MA in Holistic Health Education and Counseling, became a certified coach, and was ordained as a non-denominational Minister. In 1990, the Blessings To You Ministry was officially launched.

I loved this work because I got to give couples a voice and the opportunity to express their vision of their spirituality through their wedding ceremony! For the next 20 years, I got to be a stay-at-home and a working mom, officiate over 1000 weddings, train and coach many other officiants to do this work and coach hundreds of couples to deepen their relationships. I also got to participate in starting a charter school where I taught Spanish. Most importantly, I got to be present as a mom. Today, I know in every fiber of my being that my presence made a difference as a mom and an entrepreneur. And I am eternally grateful to the mentors and coaches who helped me along the way!

I attribute my entrepreneurial success at that time to three factors: my passion and ability to create sacred space and foster heart connections, my knowledge and experience as an entrepreneur, and mastering internet marketing. In the last ten years of that business, I learned it all: websites, search engine optimization, blogging, and eventually social media.

Fifteen years into that business, I began to feel it was time for a shift, a new workwise path. My son was approaching college, and I was exploring my next adventure. How would my gifts, talents, and skills best serve my purpose of facilitating, giving others a voice, and bringing healing to the world? I realized I could make a more significant difference in the world by teaching people who were healing the world through their businesses how to use the internet to reach more people. In 2008, I launched Whole Heart Marketing to help heart-centered, purpose-driven entrepreneurs grow their businesses and make a more significant impact.

The mission of Whole Heart Marketing is to empower and educate people on how to use internet technology to share their message, nurture relationships, grow their business, and bridge the inter-generational gap created by technology and, by doing so, further heal the planet. I'm passionate about you being seen, heard, and sharing your gifts!

Supporting heart-centered, purpose-driven women and men who were healing the world with their lives, causes, and businesses became my passion. Initially, people were growing their businesses using search engine optimization (getting found in Google searches). Later came the emergence of social media, which created new opportunities for healing and transformation. And, of course, it created obstacles as well. Now, we had to be visible, no more hiding behind our website and blog. The truth is, I was struggling to be seen and heard. All those childhood experiences of feeling powerless, silent, and invisible gave me the opportunity for a vast healing!

I became increasingly interested and excited about social media as it became more popular. However, as I got deeper into it, I started to see the ugly dark side of it. In addition, for me, social media feels like herding cats. It was confusing and overwhelming. I wouldn't say I liked it, but I knew I had to do it. I just got on Facebook to stalk my kids. Using it for business felt like a waste of time.

Like some of you, I tried to avoid it many times. I knew I needed to figure it out, and I knew I needed to be able to teach my clients. And I was struggling with it. But I couldn't walk away because even though I saw the dark side, I also saw the power! The potential! I saw the possibility for healers and thought leaders to share their message and the difference that would make in the world. One day, in my visionary brain, the lightbulb went off for me. It was about the power of the internet to reach more people through social media. I had an epiphany when someone said, "I will pass on social media. I prefer to meet people in person." I realized that for me, engaging with people on social media could have the same result as meeting someone at an in-person networking event; only I could have the opportunity to do that 24/7. It could serve as **another** networking opportunity, not to *sell* but to *connect* and build relationships and deepen connections.

We are all only 6 degrees away from everyone in the world. This means we are connected to who we know, who they know, and on and on. We are, at most, six social connections away from anyone we want to or need to meet. And in our tiny networks, we each represent at least 50K people. Whether business to business or business to consumer, you are still ultimately selling yourself, your brand, and your company to another person. And most likely, that person is somewhere on social media! **But first, they need to know you, like you, and trust you**. The current statistic is that it takes between eight to thirteen touches for you to impact someone. Social media provides opportunities for some of those touches.

I remember realizing I was "the best-kept secret with all my gifts and talents!" It was the day I stepped into my truth as a Thought Leader!

"Change happens when the pain of staying the same is greater than the pain of change." Tony Robbins

I was supporting other Thought Leaders and Changemakers when I realized I could help so many more people make a much more significant impact if I became more visible. No more hiding! I had to move past my fears, shyness, and comfort zone that was behind the scenes! It was time for me to become visible and master the art of online visibility and client attraction for myself, and now I have inspired thousands of others to do the same!!

This book is also for socially conscious entrepreneurs, people who desire to share a message, a mission, or a movement, maybe even create healing of some aspect of our world that needs healing while growing their business. My clients are authors, coaches, thought leaders, visionaries, holistic practitioners, direct sales leaders and consultants, solopreneurs, and purpose-driven entrepreneurs in service-based businesses. The common thread among my clients is that they care deeply about humanity and want to make a difference. The Internet offers unlimited opportunities to communicate and make a difference.

The strategies I teach will show you how to use social media to grow your authentic online presence, how to engage people, and how to get more eyes on your social media! You will learn what it takes to leverage the power of social media to have an ongoing stream of leads and monetize your business, book, cause, or nonprofit organization.

A successful Internet marketing strategy is determined by your target market, your message, and what you're selling. You will often see ads and hear people talk about different ways to get 10K followers in two days or be successful with Facebook Ads or whatever the latest *strategy du jour* is. Yes, those strategies might work for some businesses, but the real question is, will they work for you? My teaching strategies are meant for building relationships, referrals, and clients. If that is your goal, then this book is for you! Anybody could benefit from these strategies, and I know the strategies work for the types of entrepreneurs who want to make a more significant impact, get a message out, and grow their business.

9 TRUTHS About Social Media

The internet is a living, breathing organism. It is the total of all of us and something much more significant. As we evolve, the internet is growing. If we look at the history of the internet from the beginning, it began as a way to disseminate information. Web 1.0 started in the 1990's. It provided us with a way to find and share information. It was like an online reference directory. Web 1.0 evolved into Web 2.0 around 2005, where we could read, write, and interact! We are currently in the stage of Web 3.0 and moving into Web 4.0 and beyond. The internet may still look like 2.0, but the truth is that social media is evolving daily with more devices and artificial intelligence (AI). It is becoming more alive and dynamic every day. Here are some ways the evolution of the internet has impacted our social media activities.

TRUTH #1

Credibility is no longer for sale!

Credibility comes from influence. Influence comes from being engaged, sharing great content, and showing up consistently. You are your brand, and that is what people buy first from you. First, they decide you, and then if they will buy your service or product. Every action you take on social media leaves a digital footprint. The interactions you have, the connections you make, and the relationships you build are part of how people get to know you, and that footprint gives you credibility. The good news is that this doesn't mean you must do more on social media. It's just about doing it differently.

TRUTH #2

Numbers do not equal conversion!

Your 50K followers on social media don't mean what they used to mean. It is used to signify credibility. But most of us now know that followers don't necessarily convert to influence or monetization. You could have 5K followers and generate more influence and money than 50K. It's about who is following you.

Remember when you could buy "LIKES" on your Facebook business page? You had thousands of LIKES, so Facebook started charging you to reach those people. Maybe you even paid to get those people, but you were still not monetizing because those people were not your ideal clients.

TRUTH #3

Success is building community, more than just an audience!

Think about your own experience on social media. What are you attracted to? Wouldn't you instead connect with people authentically in a community rather than be bombarded with ads and irrelevant posts? There are now so many online opportunities to build your community, not just social media. Maybe your podcast will be the center of your community. Or perhaps it will be your blog. Social media is a great way to build your community, which will nurture relationships.

TRUTH #4

SEO-Search Engine Optimization

Every social media platform is a search engine, just like Google. With AI (artificial intelligence) helping people find what they're looking for online, searches are more accurate than ever. Your message and the words you use are more important than ever. It's not just words. It's the words your ideal clients would use to search for you. You will want to study and understand your clients' demographics and psychographics to understand their interests and what words, messaging, and images will cause them to want to engage with you.

TRUTH #5

Appearances Can Be Deceiving

You can look like you're doing everything right and not get the desired results. For example, you could be showing up, posting content, engaging, and doing all the things you think are the right things to do to attract clients, but if you're not clear about who your target market is or if your message is off, you will still miss your people.

TRUTH #6

Don't Play Follow The Leader

Just because someone else does it doesn't necessarily mean it's right for your business. For example, posting "engagement bait" is an inauthentic way of getting people to comment. This includes asking people to respond to comments by saying, "Click here if you see this post," to get more followers. Another example is related to questions. If you ask questions, ask questions that are relevant to your message.

TRUTH #7

Less is More

You don't have to be on every platform. Where you play is determined by what you're selling and who you are marketing to. You don't need to pump out tons of posts. You can build more influence and impact with one deeply thought-out, heartfelt comment or conversation than multiple posts and LIKES! Those comments and conversations offer people a way to get to know you better.

TRUTH #8

User-generated content (UGC) drives the algorithms!

This is us, the humans. We are the users, and what we do on social media is the user-generated content. This is what drives the algorithms. There are two main components to social media:

1. **Human activity-User Generated Content (UGC)**

This happens when we *play* on social media. We LIKE, comment, and share. We connect and interact with the people we is interested in building and deepening relationships with.

2. **Paid Advertising**

No one can see the ads if humans aren't playing on social media. Humans drive the algorithm by what we like, comment on, share, and post. And because we drive the algorithm, we have the power. Aside from the ads, we can choose what we click on, what we post, and what shows up in our newsfeeds. We can use social media to inspire positivity.

We are being called to evolve and become more accurate and authentic in our interactions in all the content we post. Social media is becoming more social and more about connections and relationships. We can still use the tools and opportunities for higher reach offered by social media platforms, like video, live, reels, and other forms. If you are intentional, explicit, and focused with your social media strategy, these can be powerful ways to attract your ideal clients. You attract your ideal clients as you become more authentic in how you show up.

The internet is a 24/7 opportunity to connect, engage, and discover; a**s you let go of the idea of selling, you will start to feel the difference.** You will begin to engage differently and notice that people are more willing to engage with you.

So often hear people say they don't get any clients through social media. Social media is intended for connecting, building relationships, and marketing! My definition of marketing is to inspire people to take action on what you know they need: your expertise. Most often, people find you wherever they see you, whether it's your website through an internet search, a referral from someone, or maybe they meet you at a networking event. Then they "check you out" on social media. The influence you have built through your online presence makes the initial decision for them. They decide if they will delve further into who you are or move on to someone else. So just because they didn't say they found you on some social media platform doesn't mean your social media didn't contribute to their decision to choose you. When you have developed those connections into relationships and show up consistently, you will build influence, and then a little selling is fine; you will get some results from it. **Your online presence matters because it builds influence!**

TRUTH #9

You Need to See the Value

If you don't see the value in using social media, you probably won't do it. Or you will do it halfheartedly. Take a moment right now to think about your business. What is the dollar value of 1, 5, or 10 clients over 3-6 months? Consider that and answer this question: "How much revenue could one client generate for me...five...ten?" What if you could get clients from your social media actions? Would it be worth it to you? Now, if you will, take another few minutes to think about how you could use social media to inspire positive change in the world! What is your message of inspiration and transformation? What is social media's potential for you and the people you could reach?

THE ENERGETICS OF SOCIAL MEDIA

As I became more active and excited about social media, I became overwhelmed, drained, and exhausted. Because I know everything is energy, I began to think about the power of the internet and social media. Think about your intentions around your social media. When you log on to a social media platform, you think, "Ugh! This is work! I hate this, but I know I have to do it"? Or are you logging on, thinking, "Oh yay, I get to meet some amazing people, connect with friends, see how they're doing, support their struggles, and celebrate their successes!"

It's too easy to get distracted on social media and forget the human element that you are part of a community, the human community of people playing on social media. We get distracted by all the hype, competition, **FOMO (**Fear Of Missing Out), and all the other ways we forget who we are. As we engage **with and within** this living, breathing organism known as social media, we are being energetically impacted. We are being bombarded with messages, and we are taking these messages in at multiple levels, with various senses as we see, hear, smell, taste, and sense. We also sense with our intuitive Clair senses. Our Clair sense is our ability to see visions, images, scenes, symbols, and thoughts through our third eye. You may already be aware of this, or it may be a brand-new way of thinking about social media.

These are our Clair Senses:

- Clair cognizance-knowing, intuitively
- Clairsentience-feeling through your body
- Clairvoyant-visual
- Clairaudience-auditory
- Clairgustance-taste
- Clairol faction-smell
- Clairalience-sensing odors
- Clair empathy-emotions, empathizing
- Clair tangency-feeling through your hands

I have made jokes about people posting what they had for dinner last night. But the truth is that some of us lean into the energy of that type of messaging through our Clair senses.

Are you becoming aware of any particular senses you are experiencing right now? Yes, even as you read this, digitally or in an actual book.

I began to experience social media differently once I became aware of the energetics. I noticed all the different ways I was being triggered. I started breathing into it and relaxing, and then my attitude and energy changed. I began to find that the connections I was making were deepening. The interactions were more satisfying. I was experiencing social media as a more positive way to connect and deepen relationships. I didn't hate it anymore!! I was connecting with people I had met at in-person networking events in a new way. Later on, at virtual events, too.

I started to feel the experience of the 24/7 network. You will feel differently as you begin noticing your energetic expertise on social media. You will notice things you never saw before as you travel through the newsfeeds and other people's profiles and posts.

When all of this energetics are happening, and we are on social media, experiencing them, we can become drained, confused, overwhelmed, or even anxious or depressed. You can care for yourself as you become conscious of what is happening. You can process what you are experiencing on social media differently. As you begin to notice what you are feeling, thinking, seeing, sensing, and intuiting, you can process it and empower yourself to adjust your energy. One of the ways you do this is by having a plan to find clarity, focus, direction, and intention.

Among the thousands of conscious entrepreneurs I've helped grow their online presence, a common theme is the struggle with being too visible, feeling too vulnerable and overwhelmed, causing fear and anxiety. In this book, you will learn strategies to help you be more focused and intentional. You will learn how to manage your energy on social media and how to play on social media to attract your ideal clients energetically. Whole Heart Marketing is about how you show up on social media energetically through your words, images, whole heart online presence, and bringing your whole heart essence to your online presence!

As I started to show up differently, people began to see me. They started referring me for speaking gigs to other clients, later podcasts, ezine interviews, and more opportunities for visibility. My business began to thrive! As I made these connections, I enjoyed being on social media. When I went to networking events, people would recognize me. They felt like they knew me because they had seen me somewhere on social media. I HAD INFLUENCE! And from there, I began to monetize. I built a thriving business using social media as one of my marketing strategies! Think about the potential, the possibilities, THE IMPACT **YOU** CAN MAKE!

Are you feeling a bit of a shift of possibility in using social media?

1.5

Balancing Feminine and Masculine Energies in Social Media

Another way to understand social media is through our masculine and feminine nature. In the ever-evolving social media landscape, striking a harmonious balance between feminine and masculine energies is essential. We often sense the shift but may not understand how to navigate it authentically. The call is clear - it's time to bring our *whole heart essence to our online presence.*

Feminine Aspects of Social Media
Connection and Relationship Building

Social media is a powerful tool for building connections and relationships. Prioritize genuine interactions over transactional engagements. Engage authentically on personal and business pages, creating a solid brand based on individual interactions.

Intuition and Emotional Expression

Trust your intuition in content creation and engagement. Embrace emotional expression and vulnerability for authentic communication. Emotional resonance enhances the impact of your message and fosters a deeper connection with your audience.

Community Building

Take a feminine approach to creating communities and fostering a sense of belonging. Spend significant time engaging on personal and business pages to create a supportive online environment. Communities built on authenticity contribute to a richer online experience.

Masculine Aspects of Social Media

Strategy and Structure

Strategic planning plays a crucial role in social media success. Set clear goals and define a path with intention.

Implement a structured approach to achieve your objectives, ensuring your efforts are aligned with your overall strategy.

Action and Implementation

Focus on taking action and implementing a plan. Masculine energy values leadership and authority. Establish yourself as a leader in your industry to enhance credibility and influence.

Market Yourself

Allocate a portion of your marketing efforts - sharing content that educates, inspires, and motivates. Build influence and position yourself as an expert and Thought Leader. Create a compelling call to action on your business page to inspire action, engagement, and next steps.

Promote

While promoting, strike a balance between inspiration and practical steps. Provide valuable content for free, keeping in mind the importance of engaging on a personal level on your profiles to connect authentically.

Finding Balance

Honor the fluid nature of feminine and masculine energies within yourself. Recognize and embrace individual strengths and tendencies. Collaborate and learn from both energies for holistic growth. The power lies in finding equilibrium. Elevate your social media presence by embracing both feminine and masculine energies. Building genuine connections, fostering relationships, and strategically implementing your plans will lead to an authentic, Whole Heart online presence.

1.6

Next Action Steps

A. Update your Social Media Profiles

Now that you are getting more active on your social media, you will want your profiles to reflect the most current representation of you and your brand. Make sure your profile picture is current. And that you are dressed in a way that communicates what you want to say about yourself. You want people to recognize you if they see you in person or on Zoom.

Take some time to review your "About" section, making sure everything is current. Describe your experiences and what you are passionate about, including what's in it for them!

B. Begin to Notice the Energetics of Social Media

Notice what causes you to lean into other people's social media content. Notice when you want more information and what content causes you to become curious. When do you keep scrolling by, and when do you take the next step to getting to know that person? And then think about your content. Are you creating content that causes people to lean in and get curious?

C. Explore Your Feminine and Masculine Presence on Social Media

As you think about your participation on social media, think about how you are playing on social media. Are you focused more on sharing your content, telling people about yourself and what you do, and selling? Or are you more focused on connecting with other people, building relationships, chatting, and not promoting yourself enough? Each day, as you play on social media, focus on the balance of connection and promotion.

Part II

How to Set Yourself Up For Social Media Success

"The internet is a powerful tool for positive change. Use your platform to make the world a better place." ~ Gina Rodriguez

The Whole Heart Path to Internet Marketing Success

The Internet is the great equalizer; anyone can become successful if you know what you're doing. The Whole Heart Path to internet marketing success for purpose-driven entrepreneurs requires setting yourself up for success, and it takes more than just posting on social media. It's not something that happens overnight. It requires a plan with a strategy, which takes time and effort, but the results are SO worth it! When you apply the right approach, you attract the people who are your ideal clients and referral partners, and you create a legacy online that you can feel good about no matter who finds you anywhere on the internet.

Like any relationship, you will want to nurture the relationships you attract on social media. These four steps are the foundation to create an on-going flow of leads and referrals, to powerfully master the internet to grow your mission, your movement, and your business.

1. Get personal-Create a clear message that attracts your ideal clients.

2. Get acquainted-Create a funnel, your lead magnet, and free and paid offerings.

3. Get Connected-Create your container, including your website and email marketing campaigns, to nurture the relationships.

4. Get Social-Create social media campaigns to stay connected and deepen relationships.

Step One - Get Personal

Create a Clear Message That Attracts Your Ideal Clients

Your brand is about who you are, your values, and how you want to uplift, inspire, and transform the world. How do you want to use this potent tool, the internet, for positive transformation in the world? What inspires you? What causes are you passionate about? These are great opportunities to uplift and inspire through your social media. This is what I refer to as your "core message." You will have a business core message and a personal or universal one. For many people, the core message of business and personal communication overlaps. It is like your social media umbrella. This is one aspect of your social media about you.

Elevate Your Message on Social Media to Reflect Your Brand

Now, let's talk about how to attract your ideal clients. When you log onto your social media, what's the first thing you think about? For most people, it's, "What should I say?" From this day forward, I challenge you to make the 1-degree shift. Ask a different question:

"Who am I talking to?"

"What is their struggle?"

"What is the transformation?"

Every time you log onto your social media, ask yourself, "Who am I talking to? Who is my ideal client? What do I want to share that will inspire my ideal clients to lean in to want more from me? You want them to say, "Tell me more." "He/she gets me." The internet is a whole of search engines. Your success will always depend upon your clear message, expressed with the right words, the words your ideal clients and followers would use to search for you!

What is the struggle? The better you can articulate your clients' struggles, the more they will trust you and believe you can help them. What is the struggle they express, and what is the battle you know is beneath the struggle they express? Give words to their unspoken pain and challenges.

What is the transformation? What is healing? What is the hope? There are many different levels of transformation. Share all of them.

Step Two-Get Acquainted

Let Your Ideal Clients Get to Know You With a Sample

Offer something on social media that will allow people to see how it would be to work with you. For example, if you are a coach, live, virtual training is a great way to connect with people, share some of yourself, and get to know them better. Offering a download or a quiz might not give people what they need to decide between working with you. Something where they can experience you first-hand will give them more information about you. A webinar could be an excellent free offer if you offer digital products. The difference between live virtual training and a webinar is that you are talking to the viewers in a webinar, and the interaction is via chat. In live virtual training, there can be an opportunity for more interaction and conversation.

Many people are resistant to offering something for free. It's a great way to determine the full degree of interest in your offering. Some people will always go for the free thing, but generally, this gives you the best opportunity to see who is interested in you and what you're selling. People expect something for free on social media because so many marketers have been practicing that strategy for so long, so why not try it? Look at it this way. If you were at a networking event, you wouldn't immediately start selling your product or service to each person you meet. You would take time to get to know them and determine if any of what you are selling is relevant. Then, you would probably schedule another time to chat about their needs and your services. A free offering provides you with time to get acquainted!

Step Three-Get Connected

Create Your Container to Nurture the Relationships

Now that you know what to say and where to play, let's talk about **HOW TO WIN!!** Create your container for your online presence. This includes your website, blog, and email marketing. Not everyone is ready for you right now. Email marketing helps you stay in touch with people until they are ready. You get to continue to educate, inspire, and motivate them and build and nurture the relationships.

Has this ever happened to you? You meet someone on social media, maybe in a group, and connect. You message them on a messenger app and have a Zoom call. You talk to them about working with you, and they tell you they must wait for whatever reason. You end the call, assuming you will stay connected via social media. When you go to find them, they are no longer there. Maybe their profile was deleted, or who knows what happened? They are not on your email list, so you cannot reconnect with them. Unfortunately, you're not nurturing the relationship. Down the road, a month, a few months, or a year later, you reconnect with them, and they work with someone else. Either that person was staying in touch with them, or that person appeared in their life when they were ready! It's so frustrating! That's why you want an email marketing campaign to stay in touch with people until they are prepared for you.

Don't get caught chasing the Flash Mob.

Social media is a great marketing tool, but you can't rely on it for always being there or always being the same. It's not your database, CRM, or email mailing list. There will always be a new place to play on social media and connect with people. *If you don't have your website and email marketing list, using social media is like chasing a flash mob from one social media platform to the next!* Wherever you meet people, make it a top priority to invite them to be on your list so you can stay in touch with them to continue to educate, inspire, and motivate them until they are ready for you. Your email marketing is primarily for that reason. You want to send out high-value content through your email marketing so people want to keep receiving your emails. For example, I send my blog posts out every two weeks. I send promotional emails about 10% of the time, but mainly, I send high-value content that people look forward to receiving and want to share with others.

Step Four-Stay Connected

The Whole Heart Social Media Success Formula™

Over many years of playing on social media, I have developed this tried and tested strategy for staying connected with people to nurture and deepen relationships. Read on!

50% Brand Yourself

We talked about **WHAT TO SAY.** Now that you have a clear message and know who you are talking to, let's talk about **WHERE TO PLAY.** The most powerful actions you can take on social media will be on your profile. The more of yourself you are willing to share and the more you are eager to engage with other people authentically, the more visibility and influence you will have. This is "branding yourself" on your social media.

Bring your Whole Heart Essence to Your Online Presence

You Are Your Best Lead Magnet

Everything is energy. Your intentional internet marketing aims for your ideal clients to experience the essence of who you are and what you do, visually, verbally, energetically, as close as possible to what they would experience if they met you in person. Whole Heart Marketing brings your whole heart, energy, and essence to your online presence to attract ideal clients so people feel YOUR whole heart. This is how you stand out, shine as the expert and Thought Leader you are, and get noticed. This is the most powerful use of your time on social media. Because consciously or unconsciously, people feel your energy.

Branding yourself on social media should take 50% of your time. On your social media, share yourself as much as you feel comfortable. You can test the waters to learn your limits. It's like if you worked in a corporation and it was "casual Friday" and you were allowed to wear your jeans to work, you would still be professional, just maybe more comfortable in your jeans. It's the same thing with your social media. You can be personal in a way that reflects your brand. You will want to make conscious decisions about what you share on your social media regarding controversial topics like religion and politics. When you share controversial content, it can be a distraction from your business message. If you invest your time, money, and energy into growing your business with your social media, you may not want to post content that takes people in a direction that has nothing to do with your company. Of course, it's your choice.

You can share your business on your social media. Share your passion for your business. Share what's happening and what you're excited about. Instead of thinking about posting twice a day, show up and be present twice a day, not just to share your message but to join in the conversation. Your authentic, wholehearted personal interactions will attract more people than your posts. Share other people's content as much as your own.

40% Position Yourself as The Expert in Your Field

"Marketing is inspiring people to take action on what you know they need."

Educate, inspire, and motivate 40% of your time on social media. Do this by sharing both your content and other people's content. People will share YOUR content on THEIR social media when you share engaging, relevant, compelling content. Share this type of content on both your personal and business social media. Share personal inspiration and motivation on your social media. Share your business on your business social media. For many purpose-driven entrepreneurs and Thought Leaders, the individual and business messages are very much intertwined.

When you share about your business, focus more on the transformation, why it's essential, and not so much on the "how to" because that's what you sell! Share quality content that reflects your brand and core message, articles, quotes, images, videos, and other people's content, always with your ideal client in mind.

10% Make Your Offer

Promoting your online presence is the other 10%. Share something FREE so people can get to know you!!! Share this on your business pages, with occasional social media posts.

How to "Play" on Social Media

Let's dive deeper into this! Because the internet is a 24/7 networking opportunity, with thousands of places to play, my question is, how do you show up on the internet? Do you show up as the same person you are at an in-person event? Let me give you an example. When you attend a networking event, you wear your "business" attire; maybe you affirm about meeting new people, putting your best foot forward, and bringing positive energy. You grab your business cards, and you're off to the event. Hopefully, you get your "A game."

My Networking Goals

I aim to meet people, make connections, create relationships, and have fun when I attend networking events. And in the mix of all that, hopefully, I will meet some people that I feel inclined to follow up with; we will get to know one another, develop rapport, decide that we like each other, create a new relationship that builds trust, exchange information and referrals, and get some business, new clients, new strategic partners, etc.

Here's What Happens at a Networking Event

Typically, here's how it goes at the actual event: You walk up to someone, ask them what they do, find out about them, share what you do, chat about business and non-business topics, and maybe, if it feels right, and you are so inclined, you ask for their card and permission to follow up. If it feels right, you mention your upcoming event or something going on, but only if it might be relevant to something they said.

Do you run around the room shouting, "Buy my this, buy my that?"

Hopefully, when you meet people, you don't promote, promote, promote. On the internet, networking is essentially the same as in person. The "in-person" handshake is equivalent to the hyperlink on the internet. The link connects one message to another, one person to another. You have the opportunity to make connections 24/7! Every minute, millions of links are shared, millions of internet handshakes, millions of referrals that could be referring you!!

Are you showing up consistently?

When you show up on Facebook, LinkedIn, Instagram, Twitter, wherever you are, are you consistently being who you want to be? Are you educating, inspiring, and motivating, or are you just selling all the time? Are you authentically caring about people, engaging, and interacting, or are you just looking at everyone's posts and not engaging? The Golden Rule applies online: "Do unto others as you would have them do to you." In other words, treat other people the way you want to be treated. Be authentic; don't comment and share things unless it's natural, and take the time to engage. Don't just show up when you have an event to promote. Share your best value-packed content and invest some time engaging with others!

Social Media-Do You Care?

The internet is a 24/7 networking opportunity. It offers countless opportunities to make real, authentic connections on social media. So, how's your social media going? Here are some questions for you to use to evaluate your experience: When you go to your social media to engage, do you intend to make an authentic connection? Or are you on social media to see who's doing what? Or are you on social media to tell everyone what you are up to, to get them to your next event, or to buy your product or service? Do you feel like everyone is just putting out their stuff and not caring about yours? Do you feel invisible?

The missing ingredient to your social media success might be *caring*. Maybe you are making the "LIKE, Comment, and Share," but do you CARE? I mean, do you care? Are you just doing social media because you feel like you have to? Maybe you have the dreaded FOMO syndrome (Fear Of Missing Out). You are lurking on social media because you don't want to miss out on...well, I'm not sure what. Or maybe you care about people on social media but don't know what to do or how to show that you care. You are doing "random acts of social media" with no real plan or results. What's missing in your social media is caring. I'm reminded of this quote by Zig Ziglar,

"People don't care how much you know until they know how much you care."

That's true for me. I connect with people with whom I feel an authentic connection. I'm turned off by people constantly trying to sell something to me on social media, even if it's accessible, when they have never taken the slightest interest in who I am. Sometimes, someone will send me a connection request, and less than a minute after I accept the request, they will send me a private message attempting to sell me something. It makes me want to unfriend them one minute after that!

How do you show that you CARE and make those authentic connections? Many social media coaching clients ask me, "How do I make those authentic connections?" Here is my 4-step process of authentically caring on social media.

CARE=Connect, Acknowledge, Respond, Engage

Let's say I meet someone at a networking event or a marketing speech. Here's how it might look:

Connect: Friend on Facebook, Connect on LinkedIn, Follow on Instagram, Twitter, etc.

Acknowledge: Mention on their page how great it was to meet them, interact, read their content, and comment authentically on their content.

Respond: However, they respond to you, respond, and join in the conversation authentically.

Engage: Send a private message on FB to invite them to another event you may be attending, share their content, start a discussion, and ask them for coffee or tea on Skype or in person.

Continue to remain engaged with the people with whom you resonate. Continue to stay involved in the networking opportunities social media offers you!

If you want to improve your social media results, try this next time you start to post on Facebook: *Place your hand on your heart. Take a breath in and then exhale. Relax. Start reading people's posts. Go into your heart and let yourself be guided by the person you want to connect with.* Connect on social media in the same way you connect in person. Become curious, care about them, and take the time to let them know you care. Imagine if we were all using social media to make real connections, have honest conversations, and create a fundamental transformation in the world!

What would bringing Your Whole Heart Essence to Your Online Presence look like?

Here is a challenge I offer all the time when I speak and when I teach. It's what I do! Find five new people per week to start playing with. Here are some suggestions about who to "play with" on social media.

1. Find active people.

2. Make sure their message aligns with yours. (If not, you won't want to share their content.)

3. Find strategic partners, people marketing to the same or a similar group, and sell something different. Or maybe they sell something similar, and you can refer to each other.

4. Play with other Experts, Thought Leaders, Changemakers and Industry Leaders.

5. Active networkers make great social media partners as well.

How to Play

Go to their social media platforms, personal and business. Connect with them on ALL of the social media platforms you are both on. Could you get to know them?

"LIKE," comment on, share, and CARE:

Connect with them.

Acknowledge them.

Respond to their comments.

Engage with them.

Next Action Steps

A. W-H-O

Take some time to dive deep into your ideal client's needs, wants, and interests. Each time you log onto your social media, begin your social media playtime by thinking about who you are talking to. Who is the perfect client that will resonate with your online presence? Think about their struggle and how you can help them. What is the transformation that you offer? From that thought process, connect, build relationships, and share your content.

B. Find 5 People to Play With

Choose your five people to start playing with on social media today. Whatever platform you're the most active on would be an excellent place to begin to find your people. Maybe you will find them in a group you already participate in online or in person. Start with people you know.

C. Start Engaging With Your 5 People

Once you find someone, become curious about who they are, what they do, and what you have in common. Start engaging with their social media by liking, commenting on, and sharing their posts. Give a shout-out, and give some love! Maybe even suggest a zoom or coffee connect.

Part III

Facebook?

"Social media can build bridges where walls once stood, allowing us to unite for the betterment of our world." ~ Emma Watson

3.1

Why Facebook? What is it About Facebook?

(Or any Social Media Platform)

I want to take some time to talk about Facebook because I want you to be able to make an informed and conscious decision about it for yourself. I struggled with Facebook for a long time. It's just not who I am, I thought. I'm a conscious person. I'm a spiritual, holistic coach. It's so superficial, annoying, and on and on. Here's what I discovered as I continued to explore deeper and deeper levels of my knowing: "Why Facebook??" I went through 3 rounds of "Really, Universe? Facebook?" Because I felt like it's just not who I am!! Here's the thing...

Facebook is the "Mothership"

You'll find that I focus a lot on Facebook because Facebook is the "mothership" of social media. If you use social media, I highly recommend using Facebook to the most advantage. There will always be new places to "hang your virtual shingle." Today, it's Facebook, Instagram, X, LinkedIn,

59

YouTube, TikTok, and who knows what's next? Facebook might not even be a thing when you read this book! Suppose you understand how the internet and social media work, wherever you decide to hang your virtual shingle based on your target market, messaging, and participation. In that case, you can set yourself up for success.

What's the mystery?

The mystery of Facebook is that it changes every day. Since we are all human beings as we grow and evolve, so does Facebook. It's a reflection of our society, our consciousness. This is how it can be a powerful tool for positive communication and sometimes such a harmful tool. And this is why it may evolve into something different in the future.

What's the attraction?

The attraction of Facebook is the possibility! Think about it: There are no limits to the positive opportunities to share your business and grow it on Facebook.

What's the Seduction?

Have you ever felt like, "I've fallen into Facebook, and I can't get out!" You can't stop scrolling, even though you want to. And then you start thinking, "If I just do what that other person is doing, my message will go viral!! So, what am I doing wrong?" First, you might think, or even try, "Let me just pay someone to do this for me!" I get it!! It's widespread. You are not alone! Many people deal with this by not logging on. I hope that the strategies in this book will help you focus so that when you log on, you are no longer practicing "random acts of social media with less than desirable results."

What's the addiction?

The addiction is found in the hope of finally figuring out how to "tame the beast." You keep logging on and scrolling, hoping it will be different this time, but it never is! This book will show how to use Facebook (and all social media) effectively for business. You might still become addicted, but hopefully, you will have some positive results along the way.

What's the bottom line?

Facebook is a powerful force for positive and negative change. It's not going anywhere; if it goes away, it will be replaced by a similar platform. So, we all might as well accept it and learn how to use it for good. I also want to add that although I talk about Facebook a lot, all the strategies I share in this book can be applied to all social media platforms. There will be different mechanics and demographics, but the strategy will apply to all platforms.

I'm passionate about supporting people who want to communicate their message to their community through blogging and social media. If you are reading this book, that's you! I am more focused than ever on people healing the world with their businesses. Some people need us and are waiting for our message.

The internet offers us tools for positive change, a channel for healing ourselves and the world, and a tool for Thought Leaders. Are you a Thought Leader? I am a Thought Leader who participates in the planet's healing through information, inspiration, and intuition! I signed on with the Universe and my soul to support millions of Thought Leaders to reach their people online. It sounded wild to me. First, I said 100, and then I realized I had already done that! Then I said 1000, and I felt the pounding in my heart. So, I bumped it up to 1 million. That made my heart pound even more, and it excited me. Now it's millions!! If you have a message for your community, the internet is an excellent vehicle for getting the word out! Every minute, millions of links are shared. Each time someone clicks on a link you have shared or shares it with your message anywhere on the internet, they are referring to you!!

3.2

I'm an introvert!

Most people don't see me that way because I have worked hard over the years to learn how to be visible in the world. It has not been an easy path. For so long, I felt like there was something wrong with me because I am an introvert. Why am I telling you this? If you are an introvert, feel overwhelmed by social media, and feel too vulnerable and overexposed when you are being authentic, I get it. I have had to tiptoe into social media, one message, one post at a time, testing the waters, feeling my way into how to play in a way that feels comfortable for me, and how I can feel authentic in this online world, while gently pushing myself out of my comfort zone!

I have not always been a fan of Facebook.

I have learned to love Facebook. I mean, sometimes, I hate it! (We have a love/hate relationship going on, if I'm being honest.) But most of the time, I love it because it's a way to leverage my time and energy and reach more people, to fulfill my mission to help the people who are healing the world with who they are or their businesses.

I recently realized that my success with social media evolved out of my resistance to it. When I started using social media for business, I got "tripped up" by many things. I would cringe at some of the things people posted. And I felt intimidated. I did not want to share super personal stuff on Facebook or share angry rants or endless pictures of myself. I thought that if I couldn't be on social media the way other people were, I should stay off of it.

For a while, I was a "lurker."

A lurker watches without engaging. I enjoyed checking out the people I cared about or were interested in, what they were sharing, what they were up to, and their thoughts, ideas, and musings. I figured I could bounce around, checking people out and doing my thing anonymously. (Oh, by the way, did you know that when you click on someone's page, your picture shows up higher in the images on their profile?) I guess I wasn't as anonymous as I thought. Anyway, I realized that what I was doing on Facebook was the same thing I did at networking events! I would move around the room, getting to know people, caring about them, seeing what they were up to, what they did, etc. I was actually "liking, commenting on, sharing, and caring about people" in networking events before it was even called that!

Gradually, I started to like, comment on, and share other people's posts. People began to do the same with my posts. I was getting noticed while caring about other people, and my business started to grow. My online presence started to attract my ideal clients. My influence began to increase. My business started to thrive!

3·3

Conscious Entrepreneurs—Marketing Your Business IS Life or Death

WARNING! THIS IS EMOTIONAL! IT'S ABOUT TRAGEDY! AND IT'S ABOUT HOPE!

That may seem like an extreme title, but I want to share a story with you. I'll start by saying that sometimes I think, "Wow! There's so much work to do, so many people who need help, who are unhappy, angry, sick, and full of fear. Where do I start? Maybe I'll go back to bed or find another way to keep distracted and busy and not do my work in the world." It can be overwhelming. But today changed my life, and I know I will never doubt the importance of the work I do in the world. I hope this story will leave you with the same feeling...

As I begin to tell this story, I feel my eyes well up with tears, and I have a heavy heart. It all started for me, well, for everyone involved, actually, yesterday. Yes, yesterday was one of those life-changing, life-transforming days for me. I will never be the person I was yesterday before 3:30 pm. I hope this story will move you in the positive direction it has pushed me. (I won't use real names because this is too raw).

I got up feeling a little strange yesterday morning, but I kept moving forward in my day. I was excited to go with my husband to celebrate my "soul sister's son's high school graduation. I fondly remembered my son's graduation five years ago on the drive there. Ironically, my son is graduating from college this coming Friday. Yay! I'm so proud of him.

We drove almost 2 hours to their house. We used to live 15 minutes away for 17 years until we moved three years ago. That's where we raised our son. It was so different then. Or I don't know…maybe it wasn't different. Perhaps we were just one of the lucky ones. We arrived, parked the car, and got out. I noticed a lot of commotion in front of their house as my soul sister ran up to me in tears.

"What happened?" I asked. Their long-time family friend's son had been shot the previous night. These friends live practically over the back fence from them. Their children grew up together.

"Oh my god!" After returning to my body, I asked, "How is he?"

"He's dead!" I couldn't believe what I was hearing.

Of course, the rest of the day was very surreal and challenging. It was impossible to hold back the tears. I can't tell you how hard it was to hold the duality of emotions. I was so proud of the graduate, so happy for him, and so excited for him as he was now venturing on to his next life journey while I was mourning the loss of another young person to senseless violence.

I woke up this morning trying to imagine if it was my son. How many days would I wake up, wondering, hoping for an instant, until I was fully aware that it was all a dream? My next thought was, wow, I work with all of these fantastic people, social entrepreneurs who are healing the world, one person at a time. What if that young man who shot him had gotten whatever it was he needed to keep him from ending up in that place? What do these young people need to heal their anger and dysfunction? What could have been done to help someone like him?

Do you know you are a healer in some way? There are so many ways that we heal the planet. We are all healers in our way. Are you making yourself visible and available to all the people you could be helping? I believe that each of us is an expression of the divine in a body, and we have come here to fulfill our purpose on the planet. As each of us individually heals ourselves, our families, others, and the world, there is more and more hope.

That is why I have to say it right here, right now! Marketing your business is life or death! As purpose-driven entrepreneurs, we each contribute in our own way to healing the senseless violence! Please keep going, and don't give up on yourself or the people you can help! Don't let yourself be stopped by ANYTHING! Don't ever, for one minute, think that your contribution isn't essential. Today is the day to start reaching out! It IS life or death!

I heard through the whispers and sobs that the young man who was shot was 21, in college, studying to be a teacher.

3·4

Next Action Steps

A. Reflect on Your Mission and Vision

Once you are clear with your business's mission and vision, look at your social media content. Is your social media content a reflection of your mission and vision? Are you playing with people on social media who align with your message?

B. Find a Cause to Amplify on Your Social Media

Is there a cause that inspires you? What other types of messaging could you share on your personal and business social media that align with your values and reflect who you are? Sharing a cause that matters to you is a great way to let people know who you are. I recommend steering clear of controversial topics that will create a distraction from your primary message. Only you can determine if it's on brand for you.

C.Start Increasing Your Visibility

The best way to increase your visibility is to show up more consistently. It's not so much about quantity as it is about quality. When you show up consistently, it builds trust and influence. People get that they can count on you. Join in the conversation. Remember to stay in your lane and on-brand. You will be surprised at the people who start to notice you.

Part IV

Connection, Collaboration, and Community

"Using social media responsibly can foster a sense of community and collaboration to address global challenges and promote healing." ~ Alicia Garza

Are You Playing the Algorithm Game or the Relationship Game?

You know the posts saying, "Hey everyone, type yes in the comments if you see this." Guess what! This is a hoax! Different versions seem to surface every few months, but it's a hoax. You're not being restricted. It's just that you haven't told Facebook whose posts you want to see.

Here is how Facebook (and any other platform) determines what goes into your news feed:

Facebook shows you content on subjects in which you have expressed interest. They show posts related to peoples' content you've recently liked, commented on, and shared. And they show you posts based on keywords you've used in your content. Of course, they will also show you ads that fit any interests you've expressed or the demographic categories you match.

Here's how you can determine what goes into your news feed:

In the upper right-hand corner of every post are three little dots that you can click on for a menu that you can use to tell Facebook you don't want to see that post, or you don't want to know that type of content, etc. You can check the option not to see content from a person, you can check the option not to see content from an ad, or you can check the option not to see content from a particular site that a person shares. So, you might see other content that they post, but you won't see anything from the specific site that they posted from in the post that you declined. By the way, that's how other people can also hide your content! That's why posting great, valuable content is so important, so people won't hide your content, unfollow, or unsubscribe from you! They are more likely to share your valuable content as well!

You can also go and intentionally like, comment on, and share someone's content. Then, their content will show up in your news feed because you have expressed interest in their content on Facebook or any social media platform by engaging

with them.

How to Grow Your In-Person Network Using Social Media

Social media is a great place to connect with people you meet in person, whether at networking, social events, or even people you just met on social media. Ask them if they want to stay connected on social media whenever you meet someone. As soon as possible, send them a "friend request" or "connection request." Check out their profile and business page to see what they are doing. See who their "friends" are. It's a great way to get to know people, stay connected, and deepen relationships.

Stay Connected to People on Social Media Without Being Salesy

Like, comment on, and share their content. It's just the same as a networking event. You don't want to meet someone, introduce yourself, and immediately start promoting what you're selling. You want to get to know one another. Consider joining and using other social media platforms like LinkedIn, X, and Instagram. Join a few groups. Each group has its own culture. You want to get to know and understand the group's culture before you begin participating. The first step in participating is to say hello and introduce yourself. Then, get to know people in the group.

When Do You Promote What You're Selling

Figure out when is a good time to promote what you're selling. Groups often have a particular day of the week they designate for this. If there's someone in the Facebook group with whom you think you might have a connection, you can start a conversation and then take your conversation to email, phone, or Zoom.

4·3

3 Powerful Ways to Use Social Media to Collaborate

Social Media was never intended to replace person-to-person interaction. It is a powerful way to collaborate with strategic partners to grow relationships that turn into clients. Here are three ways to do this.

Find Strategic Partners and Share Each Other's Content

Strategic partners have the same or similar target market as you but sell something different. An example would be a chiropractor, a dentist, or a business coach and bookkeeper. For example, let's say a business coach is working with entrepreneurs, helping them grow their businesses, and she knows her clients generally need a bookkeeper. The business coach would find a bookkeeper who is active on social media. They would meet, share ideas, get to know each other, and agree to share one another's posts. This is a compelling collaboration for both people.

Testimonials and Recommendations

I attend a monthly networking event where we take time during the meeting to acknowledge other people in the group whose services we have used. We thank them for the service they provided us or someone we know. You can post acknowledgments on your social media. Then, you can even ask others to share them. You can also give LinkedIn recommendations and share your and each other's LinkedIn recommendations.

Promote Events for your Strategic Partners

Promoting events for your strategic partners is another compelling way to collaborate using social media. Again, finding strategic partners, you can share invitations to each other's events and programs.

Cultivate Community Through Your Social Media

Cultivating community through your social media begins with building your online presence. Let's start with Facebook. To begin, you will want your online presence to reflect a clear, focused message so people can get to know you on both your personal and business pages. Everything you LIKE, share, or comment on in some way reflects your message. As you share content that expresses your brand, people interested in what you are up to will gravitate toward you, and your following will grow.

Start Your Community

Now that you have an online presence and a following, you can cultivate community by creating a Facebook Group. Facebook Groups offer a powerful way to connect in the community. Groups are constantly forming on just about any topic you can think of. When you set up your group, use your name and the topic in the title so people can find you by searching either category; for example, my group is called Whole

 (Please join my community!) Then, invite your friends and others interested in your group. The key to a successful group is encouraging members to participate, connect, and offer great information. You will want to get people on your list as soon as possible if something happens to your group. You can offer something free and have an opt-in form for them to give you their email address.

Join a Couple of Facebook Groups or LinkedIn Groups

Now that you have an online presence where people can get to know you and a Facebook or LinkedIn Group to join you in the community, you can find people you would like to invite to be in your community. I recommend starting with a couple of groups. Finding a great group with active participation, good conversations, and quality content sharing takes time. Once you join, get to know the members and actively participate; when and if appropriate, you can invite them to check out your group.

4.5

Social Media Can Provide You Support

Have you ever considered the power of using social media as a tool for support? Here are three ways to use social media to create support in your business!

Use Your Social Media to Create Support for Your Clients

Social media is a powerful tool that can be used to support your clients during and after a program. Create a private Facebook Group. During the program, participants can connect with you and each other. Post tips and other important information and answer questions. After the class, stay connected in the group by offering ongoing tips and tools. Participants can stay in touch with their fellow participants as well.

Use Social Media to Get Support and Feedback.

I use social media for support when I'm having a challenge. I will post my challenge on my newsfeed or in a group, and I always get many suggestions and comments. For example, I have asked for help with wording on workshop flyers, titles of events, program content suggestions, and even feedback on my headshots, logo, book titles, and covers. It's a great way to engage your followers and conduct market research.

Support People in Their Businesses by Sharing their Message

It's so powerful to support people in their businesses by sharing their promotions and content. This extends their reach. When you share someone's content on Facebook, they get a notification, and that "link love" goes a long way toward goodwill. It creates a connection that causes them to notice and remember you! And, of course, it builds influence for you! You can also use social media to support others by giving testimonials. Post the testimonial on your newsfeed, tag the person you are referring to, or add it to their LinkedIn recommendations. They will get a notification of the mention and be thrilled!!

4.6

Next Action Steps

A.Find Someone You Already know to Collaborate With

Pick someone in your lane (meaning you market to a similar ideal client, and sell something different. Maybe it's one of the five people you picked. Like, comment on, and share each other's posts. Share each other's events and promotions. Lift each other and give shout-outs. Do live and recorded interviews. You can even add more people to the collaboration.

B.Start Your Social Media Community

If you don't have a community on social media yet, start a public group on the platform you are most active on. Decide on a theme or focus for your group. Add that to the description. Start with one group. It does take some time to grow and develop, but it's worth it! This is where you can do live training announcements and connect with your followers. Invite your friends to join first. Invite people who have liked and followed you on social media. You can invite people to your group when you attend networking groups, online or in person. Whenever I speak, I invite people to join my community to ask questions and learn more!

C.Grow Your Social Media Community

Once you start a group, keep it growing! Show up consistently. Keep people engaged! Post a daily prompt, asking open-ended questions. Share live videos. Share high-value content. Avoid too much promotion, or people will leave the group. In addition to connecting and building relationships, your goal is to get people on your email list. Offer free training and other gifts to encourage people to join your list. Your email list is another way to gather your community and stay in contact with them. While social media groups are a great way to start developing a connection, you can't rely on them. Someone might leave the group, quit social media, or the social media platform might choose to eliminate the group.

Part V

Marketing

"Marketing Is About Inspiring People to Take Action On The Thing You Know They Need. Meet People Where They Struggle and Uplift and Heal Them With Your Transformation."

Stop Wasting Time On Social Media

"Facebook (or whatever platform you are trying to use) is a time suck and a waste of time!!" Does this sound like you? I hear this at least once a day from someone. And you can imagine I listen to it more than that as a social media strategist. I can save you from the depressing world of Facebook! Every day, I show people how to use Facebook to change the world positively.

Here are three things you can do today!

First, I recommend sharing your positive message of hope and inspiration. It doesn't have to be precisely about your business. It can be related to your marketing message in some way. Please share it on your profile, your business page, and any groups you are participating in. And share it on all of the social media platforms that you are on. Please share it with a beautiful picture. Try sharing inspirational quotes related to your message. What is your message? How do you want to inspire people? What is the transformation you would like to see in the world? Share about that. Notice how your social media will transform into something positive and inspiring like you!

Second, I suggest you find people who align with you to play with on social media. Who are your "strategic partners?" Who are the people attracting a similar audience to you, sharing similar values, and offering different services or products? Play with them, share their content, and connect!

Third, I encourage you to focus intentionally on your social media. Think about your intention before opening Facebook or wherever you decide to play. What is your goal? To find people of like mind to play with? To get your message out? To be uplifting and transformational? Whatever your goal is, it will be reflected in your messaging, actions, and energy; that is how you will attract connections, referrals, and clients. Many people don't get on Facebook with intention merely because they don't know where to start. They find it difficult to focus with so many options. And Facebook is changing every time you turn around, so even if you did learn how to do something on it, it might be different within a few weeks or even a few days!

That's why most people give up, just a few questions and no one to ask. Are you finally ready to make an impact and reach your people? They are waiting for you!

Taco Marketing

Marketing your message is like ordering food at a Mexican restaurant. Once you have identified and clarified your core message, you will brand your online presence through your core message. Depending on who you are targeting, you package your message accordingly. I recommend you say it in various ways to reach different people. Overall, you want all of your content on social media to be an expression of your brand and your core message; even when you like, comment, and share other people's content, you want it to align with your brand.

It's just like ordering Mexican food. You have your taco, enchilada, tostada, and burrito. It's all the same ingredients inside; the core message is the same. It's just a matter of how you serve it on the plate. Nothing has changed about your product or service. You know what you do. It's just how you communicate it. And we all know what we like at the Mexican restaurant. It's just the packaging, crispy taco shell, soft tortilla, lots of lettuce, salsa, guacamole...

This is a great analogy to use when creating your social media content. Not everyone will resonate with the same images, videos, words, etc. You don't have to change your message. After all, it's your message! You change the packaging, the mediums, and the images. You will reach different people through different images and mediums. If all Mexican restaurants were just taco stands, they would get a lot less of their target audience. But since there are so many different types of Mexican restaurants, foods, etc., the likelihood that they will reach their intended market is much higher. The next time you choose your content for social media, think carefully about whether you're communicating your message with just tacos or if you will try tostadas, enchiladas, and burritos to reach more people!

Never Too Soon *Or Too Late* to Start Using Social Media

Did you know that NOW is the perfect time for your business to start using social media? Even if your company hasn't started yet. Even if you don't quite know what you're offering or your packages and programs, you can still start growing your online presence because you have both a business and personal online presence. You can start branding yourself as a person at any time because that won't change. You are who you are. That's not going to change, no matter what you are promoting. I encourage you to use your Facebook profile for individual/business purposes. In other words, it's personal but within the boundary of how personal you choose to be, even when it's business. The more of yourself that you are willing to share, the more authentic you are and the more trust you build with people.

The statement, "People buy from people they know, like, and trust," is overused because it's true! Your potential clients want to get to know you. If you're not quite ready to launch your business on social media, you can gain followers from your online presence. Here are some actions you can take to begin growing your social media online presence now!

Set up your personal Facebook profile or whatever social media you intend to start with by adding a current and professional profile picture that aligns with your brand. Add a personal cover photo that expresses your brand (not too salty, not a banner from your website.) Fill in all the sections, including the About section. Stay connected to people you meet by asking them when you meet them if they would like to stay connected on Facebook and any other social media you have. And then follow up and connect. Start getting to know them.

Post content that reflects who you are, personally and professionally. Even if you are not posting about a specific business, you can post content about who you are as a professional leader. You can post content about what is important to you that reflects your values. Maybe your business is evolving. Post content documenting your process of developing your business. If you're writing a book, post about the process all along the way. Post quotes, articles, blogs, and videos. Find other people you respect who align with your message, and LIKE, comment on, and share their posts.

Set up your other social media platforms like LinkedIn and Instagram. Start following the friends you align with, meaning you will be willing to like, comment on, and share their content. Start doing just that. And share your content.

The next time someone says you must wait to start using social media until you are ready or it's not time yet, remember that it's never too soon to start!! You can't just use your profiles forever and never have business pages. Eventually, you will want to have a business page, populate it with great educational content, articles, and quotes, and then promote your business. And by the way, if you haven't been using social media ever or had your online presence "on hold" for whatever reason, and you realize that you are missing out on some great opportunities, it's not too late to start now!!

5·4

Your Brand Campaign on Social Media

Many times, people ask me what to post on social media. I teach people how to use social media for business, using the business page and the personal profile. You will want to have both an individual and a business campaign. A campaign is a series of actions with an intended goal. Your campaign is intended to let people get to know you in both an individual and a business capacity, what's important to you, who you are, and what you're about. Your business campaigns tell people about your business, what you do, why it's important, how it can help them, and how they can work with you to buy what you are selling.

You will always be building your campaign, in other words, branding who you are as a person. That's why you don't have to have a sales campaign to start building your online presence. It's not a waste of time because it takes time. If you start growing your online presence, when you have your business campaign ready, you launch that; people will be more likely to buy from you because they recognize you, know a little more about you, and feel connected.

Here are some guidelines for what to share on your profile if you use your social media for business. Share about the things that are important to you that are not a distraction from your message. If discussing politics and other controversial subjects is part of your brand, then go for it, but if they distract from your message, you will find that the comments and conversations on your newsfeed distract your brand. Find causes that are uplifting and inspiring.

Find people to connect with on social media that align with your brand, people who sell something different from you to a similar demographic. Like, comment on, and share their content.

Share quotes, articles, videos, images, and other people's posts that inspire you. Comfortably share your life so you feel seen and known but not overexposed.

This is what I call your Personal Brand Social Media Campaign. You are branding yourself as a person, letting people begin to get to know you so when you launch your business campaign, people feel like they know you already!

How I Use Social Media For Business

How effective is Social Networking for Business? I had the opportunity to watch a brief interview with Seth Godin, one of my marketing gurus, on YouTube. He was asked a question about how effective social networking is for business. He made a good point that if you are only in a competition to get the most "friends" and "likes" and you stop there, you will not benefit from social networking in your business. If this is what you are doing, I agree with Seth's comment that Facebook is, at best, just a fun or not-so-fun distraction, or worse, a waste of time for growing your business! Social networking is just like networking in person.

The three most important things you need to do are:

- Be real. Be authentic. Be yourself!
- Follow up with the people with whom you feel a connection.

- Create a system to record your actions so you can follow up again!

Here's one of the ways I use social media with people I have met at live events. I ask permission when I am with the person to connect with them on social media. (if I remember; sometimes I forget to ask). I then search for my new networking friends on social media and connect with them. Then, I begin getting to know them by reading their social media, website, and blog content if they have one.

Social media can be a massive waste of time. I have been there! I struggled for a long time with social media's personal vs. professional aspect. I was hesitant to put anything personal on my status because I had experienced "friends" too. I was concerned about people posting on my wall. I had my wall blocked for a long time so that no one could post on my wall.

Then, I realized that I was not being authentic. I was denying parts of my life, parts of me! I was so caught up in deciding what personal vs. professional posting level I would do that I wasn't even using Facebook. It was frustrating because I couldn't figure out what to say in my status, who to "friend" and accept a friend request from. It was making me CRAZY! It's like I was trying to figure out the rules for a game everyone else knew except me.

It became so much easier when I finally surrendered and decided just to be me, personally and professionally. That's the key: being authentic. I have a multifaceted life, and I can't classify my life into personal and professional, or I will deny some part of myself. So, for me, my social media policy is:

*Be honest, be authentic.

*Don't put anything on social media you don't want on the front page of tomorrow's newspaper!"

Since I started being myself, I have made great connections through social media, which has benefited my business!

How to Get More Followers and Fans

Whenever someone "FOLLOWS" a page, blog, post, etc., the link appears in their feed so all their friends and followers will see it. This is a potent viral marketing tool. Here are some powerful ways to get people to follow your Facebook Page or any other social media.

If you have just launched your page, didn't do this when you launched your page or didn't do this in a while, post in your "status" that you have just launched or re-launched your page and would like them to follow you. Say something like, "I just launched a Facebook page for my business. Can you please click on this link and follow my page? Thanks." (Don't forget to include the link.)

Send an email to everyone on your list. You can ask them to follow your page, etc. Include the link to your page. Include a "follow me on social media" note with links to your social media pages in your email signature. Each time you send an email, you can ask them to follow your post, page, etc., in your signature.

Include the link to your page. Suggest that your friends follow your page. (This is a more indirect approach; you suggest a page vs. asking them to follow it.)

Invite people to follow your page. Here's how you do that: Go to the Facebook page you want people to follow. You will see an option to "invite friends." If you can't find it, just Google, "How do I invite friends to follow my business page on Facebook?" I would give you instructions, but they will most likely not be accurate when you read this!

Start choosing friends by typing in names or select from the ones that come up by clicking on "invite" at the bottom of the page. Once you click on the "invite" option, Facebook will send an invitation to everyone you choose, with your link, suggesting you page. Hopefully, they will follow your page. There is a limit to how many people you can select at one time, but you can do it again. I recommend waiting about a week after you "friend" someone before you invite them to follow your page. Take time to get to know them so it doesn't feel too salesy.

Remember that social media newsfeeds are live feeds; they change constantly, so people will not see every post and status you share. Therefore, putting the same link out once a week is acceptable while trying to get people to follow your page. Just change the content of your message. I would recommend once a week for a couple of weeks. Then, take a break. Feel free to do it again. If you find that someone didn't follow the page after you invited them, you can message them via Messenger if you feel comfortable doing that. I recommend that only if you know the person and have some relationship with them. Maybe they didn't see the invite or forgot to respond.

Take These Actions on Social Media to Engage Your Followers

Are you struggling with your Social Media? Technically, you know how to do it, but you're not doing it. You get ready to post something, put your cursor on the send button, start to click, and then suddenly find yourself clicking over to someone else's wall to see what they've posted. You wonder if what you're posting is similar, different, OK, proper, wrong, or going to embarrass you or someone else? Is it something you want out there on the internet forever? Wow! That's an even bigger question! Well, no wonder you're struggling, stuck, not doing it! Wasting time! Frustrated!

Here are three actions you can take on your Social Media with confidence.

You will never have to hesitate or worry about doing something wrong or making a mistake. You can do this from your personal or business social media. This is a great strategy to stay consistently visible on social media.

Inspiration

You can always post inspiring quotes and images. When you search for content, use your keywords. Keep your brand in mind. If your brand is positive and uplifting, post positive and uplifting content. You can also share other people's inspiring quotes and comment on them when you share them.

Share Your Blog

Your blog is intended to educate, inspire, and motivate your potential customers. It's not about promotion. When you share your blog on social media, share a couple of engaging sentences, a great image, and a link to your blog post on your website. The image doesn't have to be on your blog post on your website. I share different photos with each of my social media snippets because different images attract other people. Although social media platforms prefer that you do not lead people off the platforms, I still recommend you put the link back to your site with your blogs. Suppose you follow the Whole Heart Social Media Success Formula™, 50% interacting, engaging, 40% great educational content like quotes, images, videos, and your blog.

In that case, it's acceptable to share the link to your blog once or twice a week on your business social media. I share the link only once profile, who

Like, Comment, Share, and CARE

When in doubt, you can always LIKE, comment on, share, and CARE about other peoples' content relevant to your brand and marketing message. And you will be appreciated!

5.8

Next Action Steps

A.Personal Social Media Campaign

Your social media campaign is how you brand yourself. It is about letting people get to know you. You can share inspiration and things happening in your life that are not too personal cause you are passionate about them. Share your passion for your business, what excites you, what you love, and what you love about how you work with your clients. Open a new document on your computer or take out a piece of paper and start brainstorming ideas for topics for content on your profile.

B.Business Social Media Campaign

Your social media campaign educates, inspires, motivates, and promotes your business. Post content that will create curiosity and cause people to want more from you.

C.On-going Social Media Campaign

This is an ongoing campaign that never stops. Even if you are on a break from your business or not selling anything at the time, you want to stay present on your social media. Post someone else's content if you're not feeling inspired or unsure what to post.

Part VI

The Power of Blogging

"Our digital voices have the power to spark real-world change and healing. Use them wisely." ~ Brittany Kaiser

Why I Blog

I blog because it's a way to reach my people, my tribe, with my heart. I admit that many of my posts don't appear to be from my heart because I often blog about technical aspects of blogging, social media, SEO and internet marketing. Whenever a client asks me a question about how to do something related to what I teach, I write a blog post. If one person asks, there are 10 or 100 who also want to know the answer! It's all from my heart. I am passionate about teaching internet marketing strategies, and that's from my heart!

What Will I Talk About

Last night, I attended a networking event and started chatting with a woman entrepreneur about blogging. She said she had no idea what to blog about. Have you struggled with that question? She is like so many people who are stopped before they even start with the thought, "What will I talk about?" There are other versions of that thought, too, like "I'm not a writer," "Who will want to read what I've written?" and so on!

She owns a consignment store with so many different types of excellent, unique, and even exceptional items. I shared with her about another client I had worked with who was selling designer ties on eBay. Her tie sales were going pretty well, so I recommended that she start writing a blog post about some of the designer ties. Every time she wrote a post about a tie, that tie would sell, and her overall sales would increase. Even if the tie she wrote about had been sold, it brought people to the site, and they purchased other ties!

Blog About your Products and Services

I suggested to the consignment shop owner that she start blogging about some of the items in the store, telling stories about them, describing them, and talking about the store through the inventory. I recommended that she choose items from her main categories of items in the store. That way, even if the items she blogged about were sold, other items would still be in that category for people to purchase. I told her that if she got any "brand name" new or newer items, she could blog about those as well. No matter what product you are selling, there is always a story about the product, about people using the product, experiences, and testimonials.

If you sell a service, it's no different than a product. Talk about your services, stories, experiences, and testimonials. Give examples. The more you can share about it, the more people will lean into what you are blogging about. It's essential to stay away from promotion. Stick to sharing about your services with examples.

You Are a Writer!

Seeing the light bulb go on for her was terrific when I shared about the ties and how she could find unlimited ideas to blog about from her inventory. She realized she had something to write about, and now she can launch her blog and feel excited about it. I have often observed that the "I'm not a writer" comment is more about not knowing what to write about when it comes to blogging.

Creating Credibility Through Your Blog

Maintaining a blog will be a massive contribution to your success. That credibility drives readers to learn more, engage, form opinions, and even make decisions. Put, blog credibility keeps your readers coming back for more of your posts and updates. And it gives people a sense of familiarity with you. Your blog leaves people feeling like they know you. They feel connected to you.

So, how do you ensure your blog's credibility? First, ensure you're blogging about something you love and know much about. You will find that the more you know about something, the easier it will be to write about. Furthermore, because you love it, you'll be motivated to update your blog regularly and find new things to write about.

Make sure your content is highly informative and high-quality. For instance, if you're doing a food or craft blog, it will help your followers greatly if you include photos and videos to give them a better idea of what you'd like to share. If you're sharing your opinion on a relevant news story, you may want to include a link to an official news video or article on the issue you are commenting about. Having content like this on your blog makes it much easier for your followers to see your point of view and maybe get encouraged to share their opinions through comments. And if you're sharing about a service, give enough information so people can understand how it would be for them to experience the service you provide (of course, without selling). You can do this through examples, stories, and testimonials.

Let's talk about comments. I recommend adding social media "SHARE" buttons to the blog and keeping comments closed on your website. This will encourage people to share your blog on social media and comment where more people will see the comments. Take the time and care to reply to your readers' comments and questions. This helps build the interactive part of the blog by involving your readers in discussions, bouncing ideas off each other, and ultimately making a connection. Some readers may share your replies or recommend your blog to their friends if they see you are attentive to their opinions.

Blog credibility is a great thing to maintain; it takes a reasonable amount of work. It may sound like a lot to do right now, but once you get it started and get the hang of it, and you start to see the return on your investment, it'll be worth it.

6.3

How to Simplify Your Blogging

Blogging is not meant to be tedious because it's a relatively relaxed form of writing, but some people encounter difficulties maintaining blogs. If you're one of them, here are a few valuable tips.

Keep a Pen and Paper Handy

You never know when inspiration could strike, so always have a pen and a small notebook ready where you can write down anything interesting that crosses your mind anytime, anywhere. This way, you can return to that inspiration when you're finally in front of your computer and ready to blog away.

Create a List of "Keyword Phrases"

If you're doing SEO (search engine optimization) for your blog, it's best to create a list of keywords you will likely use. These are phrases that your ideal clients would use to search for you. Find the best two keyword phrases, primary and secondary.

You don't want to or need to overuse them in your blog. Use your primary keyword phrase in either the title of your blog or the first sentence, and then use each keyword phrase a couple more times.

An easy way to determine effective keyword phrases is to imagine you are your ideal client, searching for the service or product you offer. Please make a list of keyword phrases you think they might use. Then, search for these words in Google to start. If the results are related to what you are selling, then it's a good keyword phrase. If the results are not related, keep searching. Search the websites of leaders in your industry and see their most used keyword phrases based on the content on their website pages. Always test in Google to see if the results are relevant to what you do.

Schedule Time to Blog

It's always wise to set a schedule. If you don't add your marketing tasks, including time to write your blog posts, into your schedule, it's too easy to skip them. You can add time to your schedule to work ON your business, and then if something comes up, you can always reschedule that time. Reschedule it immediately so it doesn't fall through the cracks.

Encourage Guest Posts

Guests' posts are constructive if you're preoccupied with other things or feeling burnt out. To ensure the quality of guest posts, set precise requirements so you won't feel bad rejecting a poorly written submission.

Guest posts are also a great way to promote your blog. Ask your guest to share the blog after you post it. You can gain a whole new group of followers that way.

Ensure the content you put on your blog, or if you are a guest blogger on someone else's blog, is original. You do not want to have the same content on two different websites. If someone sees one of your blogs and wants to add it to their blog and give you credit, you will want to write an original blog for them instead. It can be similar but not the same.

Repurpose Past Posts

If you're busy and do not have guest posts, you can always re-purpose a past post. Write it in a new angle, make it timely if applicable, and add elements you originally left out because it made the post too long for comfort. If the old post was all text, maybe you can add a photo now. Add a new story, example, or testimonial.

Don't Think That You Are Blogging

When blogging, sometimes we get too focused on what the readers might think about our posts. Will they like it? Will they be amazed? Or will they find something wrong with it? People will always have something to say, be it good or bad. Sometimes, it helps to forget that you are blogging when you are blogging. It takes the pressure off your shoulders and lets you enjoy your work. Don't forget blogging is supposed to be fun.

6.4

Get Your Blog On

The first step to your successful online marketing plan is to "Get Your Blog On." This means starting a blog. Having a blog allows you to express your humanity online. It will enable you to create relationships with your clients and potential clients. It also allows you to position yourself as an expert in your field, sharing your expertise freely.

Before you start to blog like crazy, I recommend figuring out what your blog will be about. Having a focus for your blog will help you reach more people. That may seem backward, but here's how it works. If you blog about everything under the sun or several different subjects, you will reach some people with each subject, maybe. The sad truth is that you have about 2 seconds to grab someone once they land on your page. If someone lands on your blog and it's not what they are looking for, they will bounce off of your site and might not return. Sometimes, you only get one chance to grab someone that lands on your site. If they land on your site and it's what they were looking for, they will stay longer, read more, and even take action on your site, like sign up for your "free report" or subscribe to your blog.

Build an Email List

The second step to your successful online marketing plan is to build an email list. This includes a few things. Keep blogging. Keep sharing your blog. And create a list. Build a list with an email capture and list-building program like A Weber or Mail Chimp. I have used A Weber for quite some time now. (I am an A Weber affiliate, so if you decide to try A Weber and click on the link, I will receive a small commission each month.) I have used MailChimp, A Weber, and Constant Contact and found A Weber to be the most user-friendly and functional for building and keeping in touch with my list.

Blogging is a great way to build relationships with people who don't know they need you or aren't ready for you yet. You can continue to educate and inspire them until they are prepared by getting them on your list. If you set up an email capture program, you can encourage people to subscribe, build a list, and then keep in touch with the people on your list very easily. You can send them your blog posts and other information you have as it comes up.

Get Your Blog Moving

The third step to your successful online marketing plan is to "Get Your Blog Moving." In other words, get your blog out to the world via social media and other online avenues like guest blogging and affiliate partners. Having a blog is great, but if you don't share it regularly, not many people will benefit from your wisdom and expertise. You will remain "the best-kept secret."

Blogging and using social media effectively is one of the fastest, most potent, most effective, and least expensive ways to position yourself as an expert. I have to admit I resisted blogging for a long time. Here's why I resisted:

1. It takes so much time

2. I don't have enough to write about

3. Who will read it?

4. What do I have to say?

5. What do I do with it after I write it?

6. Where do I start?

7. If I give away all my information on my blog for free, why will people want to pay me?

The more you write, the more you discover what to say! People will read it on your site. People searching for a solution to the problem you solve will find your content when they search. And when you give people so much value for free, they want to pay you! What's your reason? If you're not blogging, why not? If you're blogging and reaching your people, YAY!! Keep on Blogging.

7 Reasons to Embrace Blogging

Anyone Can Create One

Anyone can write a blog post about anything they want. Everyone has a voice, and the best voices will rise to the top. You, as the writer, can show your personality. In blog posts, you have more leeway to add to your voice and personality than other types of writing.

Blogs Are a Great Way to Communicate Your Expertise

You can help people, learn new things, and entertain your audience—endless and unique possibilities. Blogging opens up all of these to a vast audience.

You Can Grow Your Community

Blogging allows you to connect with other individuals who share the same interests. Sharing your ideas, inspiration, wisdom, and expertise through your blog attracts people of like mind to grow your community. As you begin posting your blog posts, you will notice more intentional conversation around your well-written blog.

It's Good for SEO

By keeping content on your site fresh and relevant, you can use your blog to boost the search engine ranking (SEO) of your site and your business. Every time you post a blog, your website notifies the search engines and becomes a current website instead of a static one, and therefore, it is more likely to be brought up in search results.

It Brings People Back to Your Site

If your blog is value-driven and updated regularly, people will return looking for more and bring traffic back to your site.

It's Free

It costs zero dollars to post to the blog, so if you have something to say, nothing will stop you.

You Can Establish Yourself as a Thought Leader

A blog is an excellent place to share your original thoughts and can be an excellent way to showcase your individuality. This is how you become a Thought Leader in your industry!

Next Action Steps

A. Find a Blog That You Love

Decide on a topic that interests you. Consider a topic that would be relevant to your ideal clients so you can share the posts on your social media as you follow and read the blog. Once you determine a topic, search Google for related blogs and pick one. Notice what you like and don't like about the blog. Do you like the way it's written? How about the formatting? Length of the paragraphs, font size, pictures, or no pictures. All of these aspects of the blog are relevant and will contribute to whether someone chooses and reads your blog.

B. Brainstorm Blog Topics For Your Blog

Explore topics that your ideal clients would be interested in. Start with the ten most frequently asked questions. Write a blog about each of these. Then, write a blog about each of the ten questions you wish your ideal clients would ask you. Most people don't know enough about what we do and how we can help them, so this is an excellent approach to educating your ideal clients.

C. Write Your First (Or Next) Blog Post

Start with one blog, 375 to 500 words, 6 to 8 paragraphs. Write your blog in a conversational tone so it's easy to read. Please keep it simple: 3 key points and some takeaways. I recommend that your blog posts are educational and inspirational. You will have other opportunities to promote. Post your blog on your website and social media for extra credit. Notice the response to your blog on social media.

Part VII

Use Social Media to Inspire and Motivate

"Social media allows us to connect with others passionate about healing the planet, creating a community of change-makers." ~ Ellie Goulding

Grow Your Brand and Leadership Legacy Online

What is Your Legacy Online?

What do you want people to remember about you, your message, your mission, and your movement, online and offline? Your Thought Leader Legacy is about you as a person and your mission! It's also about your business.

Think about your brand. What do you want people to experience when they land on your website, your social media platforms, or when they see your message in their social media newsfeed?

We are all Thought Leaders in different ways in our lives! Some of us have more followers than others. You're making an impact with everything you do on the internet, including your social media, so be intentional. You are creating a lasting brand online. Every action you take on the internet leaves a digital footprint. Consider the path of your digital footprint with every step you take. Show up as the Thought Leader that you are through what you LIKE, comment on, share, who you follow, connect with, "friend," and interact with. It all shows, and your followers are watching you. This is a powerful way to elevate your leadership brand and reputation online and create a lasting legacy of who you indeed are.

Marketing is About Inspiring People

Marketing is not sales! How many times have you heard that? But it's so true, and we often forget it. I hear people say, "Ugh! I hate marketing!" But I think what they struggle with is sales. By this, they mean, "I don't like feeling pushy, salesy, and icky!" And that's a different conversation. What do I mean by "Marketing is about Inspiring People?" When you create content for your and potential customers, you want it to be inspiring. You are attempting to educate, inspire, and motivate people to take action. Of course, the action you want them to take is related to your expertise, but it's not about sales.

You are creating content to attract the people who will benefit from your expertise. These people are ready to learn, buy from you, and benefit from your products and services. Maybe they are prepared to purchase from you, but you don't know that, and neither are they. When they see your posts in their newsfeed or land on your social media, you want them to "lean in" and say, "Tell me more."

Let's say you are a health and nutrition consultant, and you are passionate about inspiring people to eat right. You want to motivate them by offering information about how to eat right, what to eat, what not to eat, the results of not eating right, and the benefits of eating right. In your blog, you're not selling them your workshop, webinar, or even your products. You're inspiring them to take the "right action." You will have tools and programs to support them, but that's a different conversation.

Your content, including your blog, intends to educate, inspire, and motivate people and build relationships. Hopefully, what people get from all of your content is a good feeling about you, a feeling that you care about them and want to help them. They get to know you and what you're passionate about. If they feel this, they will take the following steps to learn more about you. If every one of your blog posts or social media posts ends with "buy my this or that," people feel pushed, and they usually don't buy your "this or that." But when they think you genuinely care about them, they are inspired to act.

Social Media is a Powerful Tool for Visionaries and Thought Leaders

Many people, including conscious Thought Leaders, shy away from social media because they experience it as superficial and a waste of time. As mentioned, it can be superficial, and it can be used for harmful purposes. Here are some suggestions to transform your social media activities into decisive actions that reflect the Thought Leader you are!

Your Core Message

Think about your core message. What do you want people to grasp from your social media messaging? Be intentional with your words whenever you get ready to LIKE, comment, share, and post. Share content that will resonate with your ideal clients. When you share wisdom, stories, and experiences they can relate to, it gives people hope. You are using your social media to lead them to the possibility of transformation in their lives, the transformation you offer.

The People You Play With

Who do you "play" with on social media? Are you engaging with people whose message aligns with your core message? Do you share the same values with those whose content you like, comment on, and share? Are you following people whose followers are the people you want to reach? Are they also Thought Leaders? Find people to play with on social media who actively use it as a transformation tool.

What Are You Sharing?

Think about the people you want to reach. Share your inspiring and educational message so they feel like you "get" them. You want them to feel a sense of relief as they read your social media posts, that you understand their challenges, and that help and hope are there for them to experience positive transformation. Use your social media to make a positive impact!

7.4

Use Social Media to Envision a Brighter Future

The Internet is a powerful force for positive change in the world. **Marketing is Life or Death—Share Your Message of Transformation on Social Media!** Does what you do save lives? If you are a healer of any kind, you save lives. Your people need you! You might die inside if you are not getting your heart message out to your people. I believe we have reached the time when we must own who we are and what we came here for to do our soul's work and be willing to shout it from the rooftops. Share how people are transformed by the work that you do. Share stories of transformation.

Our Younger Generations Need Our Wisdom and Inspiration—Share Hope

You have an opportunity on social media to share whatever you want. Often, I hear people say they don't know what to share or are overwhelmed by being on Facebook. Here are some suggestions. Share your message of hope and inspiration. Share other people's messages of hope and inspiration. When you read people's social media posts, share what touches your soul, brings a tear to your eye, or joy to your heart. Think about the positive footprint you want to leave on the internet and let yourself be heard through that filter.

We Need the Inspiration and Wisdom of Our Younger Generations—Encourage Them to Share Their Message

The internet has caused an inter-generational gap. It can be a bridge, or it can separate further. If you're of that age when *you weren't born with a mouse in your hand*, you may not get social media. I encourage you to approach social media as the powerful tool that it is. Look for things to LIKE, comment on, and share that reflect your vision, values, and message. Look to people from the younger generations on social media who are Thought Leaders and visionaries and share their messages. If you look for them, you will find them! And encourage them whenever you can to share their positive message!

How Social Media Can Help You Achieve Maximum Influence

Building influence on social media involves caring about others and sharing your message. We all want to feel seen and heard. Here are the three C's of growing your online presence to build influence that will bring your ongoing referrals and clients.

Content

First, think about content—yours and other people's content. You will build influence if your online presence authentically reflects you and your core message, in other words, your mission. For example, my mission is to empower and educate people on how to use internet technology to share their message, nurture relationships, grow their business, bridge the inter-generational gap created by technology, and further heal the planet. What is your mission, your core message? When you share your content and when you LIKE, comment on, and share other people's messages, share content aligned with your core message.

Consistency

Social media is a 24/7 networking event. Like any networking group, if you want to build influence with your online community, show up consistently with your brand and message so people can grow to know, like, and trust you. Consistency also includes a healthy balance of visibility and engagement. Share your content and engage with others.

Connection

Social media provides unlimited opportunities to connect and build relationships that turn into referrals and clients. Connect with people personally by going beyond liking to engage in a conversation. I've talked about my Whole Heart Social Media Success Formula™. Implement it for Maximum Influence:

Authentically engage with your online community (50%)

Share your education, information, inspiration (40%)

Promote your products and services (10%)

Build your influence with these three C's. The more influence

you have, the less you need to promote!

7.6

Share Your Message

When you write your blog, share your message. Answer the questions your clients ask you all the time. Answer the questions your clients should ask to understand more about what you do. Your blog gives you more time to explain what you do, how you're different, and what the experience of working with you will be like. Share high-value information and avoid promotion.

Share your message through other people's content.

Social media offers many opportunities to share other people's content, but you must share content that reflects your brand. Sharing funny or controversial things is tempting, but make sure it reflects your brand. If your brand is a little edgy, then by all means, share edgy. If your brand is about positivity and motivation, those are the types of posts you can share from other people's content and your own.

Inspire your followers with your message of inspiration.

I encourage you to share quotes and articles that will inspire and motivate people to take action on your expertise. Make sure whatever you share is in alignment with your values. If everything you share aligns with and reflects your values, then people will know who you are, know what to expect from you, know who to refer to you, and see if you are a good match for them.

Connect with people who reflect your message.

Do some research on social media about whom you might connect with. This should be someone who has similar potential clients but offers different services. Hopefully, they will share content that reflects your values. You share their content; they share yours, and everybody wins!

Next Action Steps

A.Think About Your Thought Leader Legacy Online

Your content, what you share, and who you like and comment on reflects your values. What matters to you? What are some topics you could share that will inspire others? Some topics might be beauty, love, freedom, and joy. These topics are more significant than your business message, although they may encompass your business and personal message. Get out the pen and paper or the document and start making a list of topics so you are prepared with some great ideas next time you have an opportunity to post.

B.Start Using Your Social Media to Envision a Brighter Future

How can you use your social media to envision a bright future? How can you inspire others? Thinking about your values and beliefs and your business mission, what could you share to inspire hope in others?

C.Find and Post Content That is a Reflection of Your Core Message

Now that you have some topics, search Google for content expressing your message. Look for people sharing content your ideal clients would resonate with.

CONCLUSION

"Social media is the ultimate equalizer. It gives a voice and a platform to anyone willing to engage." ~ Amy Jo Martin

There is so much more to say, and in the spirit of "Less is More," I am choosing to conclude with the last chapter. My book aims to give you tools and strategies to take a leap into becoming more visible. In the previous 17 years of teaching heart-centered, purpose-driven entrepreneurs, I have seen that even though many have the tools and are on social media, they have not achieved the level of visibility and influence that is possible. I offer you inspiration and motivation to take the risk to step out and start showing up online even more than you already are as your most authentic self and shine as a Thought Leader! You have opportunities to network, connect, share your whole heart, essence, message, mission, and movement, build influence, and create the positive change you wish to bring to this world through your work and who you are!

Wholeheartedly,

Diana

ABOUT THE AUTHOR

Diana Concoff Morgan, Marketing Strategist, #1 International Best Selling published author, and national speaker, is a successful entrepreneur with over 35 years of experience building two successful businesses using the strategies she teaches her clients.

The mission of Whole Heart Marketing is to empower and educate Thought Leaders and Changemakers, including speakers, coaches, authors, holistic practitioners, healers, and other entrepreneurs, on a mission on how to master internet technology to:

Leverage the power of the internet to grow a sustainable business and life;

Cultivate increased Communication, Connection, and Community among all people everywhere;

Create your Brand and Legacy online so you can Shine as an Expert and Thought Leader;

Bridge the inter-generational gap that has been created by technology.

The Whole Heart Marketing Strategy is designed to increase connections and transform them into referrals and clients with tried and tested strategies. Diana has passionately helped thousands of entrepreneurs grow their businesses, specializing in training to Master the Art of Online Communication, Networking, and Client Attraction. She brings 35 years of experience to her clients, including business development, sales, marketing, advertising, internet marketing, website development, SEO, blogging and social media, comunication mastery, coaching, and spirituality.

She understands the challenges of building a strategic and authentic online presence that will reflect your *whole heart* message, create your Thought Leader legacy online, and bring you the right clients on an ongoing basis. She has the patience and know-how to help you. Whole Heart Marketing offers various strategic consulting services, coaching programs, live virtual training, and self-paced courses.

LEARN HOW TO CREATE YOUR WHOLE HEART PATH TO PROFIT

Diana offers 1-1 consulting, coaching, and group programs. She teaches entrepreneurs how to grow an authentic and monetizable online presence, including a clear message, an effective lead magnet, powerful email marketing, intentional social media marketing, delegation, and what and how to delegate to an assistant. After running her own "Done For You" company for 14 years, she realized that teaching her clients how to do this process themselves would be more beneficial, so she created the Whole Heart Path to Profit System. Her duplicatable "business in a box" approach has helped thousands of entrepreneurs understand what it takes to monetize on social media so they can then hire their assistants and know what to expect from them.

LET'S STAY IN TOUCH

Diana@wholeheartmarketing.com

925-980-9052

www.WholeHeartMarketing.com

https://www.facebook.com/WholeHeartMarketing

https://www.linkedin.com/in/dianaconcoffmorgan/

https://www.instagram.com/dianaconcoffmorgan

https://twitter.com/dianarcmorgan

https://www.youtube.com/dianaconcoffmorgan

https://www.pinterest.com/dianacmorgan/

HIRE DIANA TO SPEAK

https://wholeheartmarketing.com/speaker/